A Place of
Quiet Rest
Journal

"Nothing can compare to the joy and privilege
of sitting and learning at the feet of our heavenly Master."

Nancy Leigh DeMoss

MOODY
PUBLISHERS
THE NAME YOU CAN TRUST®

ISBN: 0-8024-6646-X
EAN/ISBN-13: 0-8024-6646-4

1 3 5 7 9 10 8 6 4 2

Printed in the United States of America

From My Heart to Yours

I have often said that if I could share just one message with women, it would be on the importance of a personal devotional life.

It's not that there aren't other important truths that need to be communicated —I have addressed many different topics through *Revive Our Hearts* conferences, daily radio programs, and publications. But I really believe that the most helpful thing I can do for the women I minister to is to get them into the Word of God for themselves. I'm convinced that if women will get to know God through His Word, sooner or later, God will show them what they need to know in order to deal with their most difficult issues and how to live godly, fruitful, blessed lives!

For years, I looked for a good resource I could recommend to women who wanted to learn *how* to have a daily quiet time. I found (and have used) many wonderful devotional books, but could not find a book that explained how to actually develop a personal devotional habit. It was to help meet this need that I was prompted to write my first book, *A Place of Quiet Rest*. What a joy it has been to see how God has used that book to draw thousands of women into a more intimate relationship with Himself.

A 30-Day Challenge

Whenever I have spoken on this subject, I have been encouraged to discover how hungry many believers are for a more consistent, meaningful devotional life. But I've also seen that most people feel overwhelmed with their existing schedule—they need a jump-start to help them develop the habit of carving out time in their day to spend alone with the Lord.

One of the most practical means I have found to help busy people develop a consistent devotional life is a simple "30-Day Challenge." Rather than encouraging people to make a lifetime commitment to have a daily quiet time (a commitment they will most likely not keep for very long), I have challenged them to get started by making a commitment to *spend some time alone with God in His Word and in prayer, every day, for the next thirty days.*

I have given this challenge to hundreds of thousands of women in recent years, and have been thrilled to see how God has used this commitment to make a world of difference in the lives of tired, needy believers who long to know God in a more intimate and real way. Here are some of the kinds of comments I have received from those who have taken the 30-Day Challenge:

> *A truly phenomenal experience . . .*
> *My life has been beautifully transformed . . .*
> *When I started, 15 minutes seemed too long, but now two hours isn't long enough! . . .*
> *It's been more than 30 days, and I don't want to stop! . . .*
> *I've been revived! . . .*

I don't know where God finds you at this juncture. The whole idea of a daily devotional life may be new to you. Or perhaps, you have started—and quit—and many times started again, only to quit once more. Or you may already be enjoying consistent time alone with God each day. Wherever you are, I want to encourage you to go further, to press deeper into an intimate relationship with God.

Over the years, whenever I have spoken on the devotional life, I have closed my message by asking this question: "How many of you would be honest enough to admit that you do not currently have a consistent personal devotional life?" I have asked this question in scores of settings—with groups of lay people, Bible study leaders, and full-time Christian workers. Invariably, 80–90% of those in the room raise their hand, acknowledging that they are not currently having a regular quiet time.

I always follow that question by inviting people to take the 30-Day Challenge. What a joy it has been to see many thousands of people stand to their feet, signifying their commitment to *spend some time alone with the Lord each day—for the next thirty days.*

A Personal Invitation

If you are not currently enjoying a consistent devotional time with the Lord, the 30-Day Challenge may be just the place for you to start—or get started again.

You may be wondering how you can possibly add "one more thing" to your already overcrowded schedule. Let me assure you that if you will make knowing God the #1 priority of your day, God will show you how to fit everything else into your day that is on *His* "to do" list for your life!

Spending time alone with the Lord each day has become an absolute necessity for me; it is one of the richest blessings of my life. That doesn't mean it's always easy— in fact, the enemy fights me on this one virtually every day! But I have determined that this is a battle worth fighting, because I know I cannot be the woman God made me to be—nor can *you*—apart from spending time each day in His presence.

This journal is your invitation to take the first step. Are you ready to take the 30-Day Challenge? If so, I'd encourage you to sign below as an expression of your commitment to the Lord.

By God's grace, out of a desire to know Him more intimately,
I purpose to spend some time alone with the Lord
in the Word and in prayer,
every day for the next thirty days.

_____
SIGNED

_____
DATE

Once you've made that commitment, expect that the enemy will do everything he can to hinder you from keeping it! If you miss a day, *don't give up!* Simply purpose by God's grace to keep on going. My prayer is that the 30-Day Challenge will become a life-long pattern and priority for the rest of your life, and that your life will bear the sweet fruit of an intimate love relationship with Him.

Warmly,

Nancy Leigh DeMoss

How to Use This Journal

The purpose of this journal is to help you develop a more intimate and consistent relationship with the Lord. As was the practice of Jesus, and men like Moses, Joshua, David, and Daniel, I would encourage you to meet God early in the day—while it is still quiet and your mind is free from distractions. Whatever time of day you choose, find a solitary place and make sure you have your Bible, a pen, and your journal.

I have found that my time with the Lord is generally more meaningful (and my mind less prone to wander) when I record what God shows me in my time with Him. This journal is designed to help facilitate that process.

The journal is divided into thirty days, each of which includes an inspirational quote about the personal devotional life, as well as the following elements:

PREPARING MY HEART

Take time to quiet your heart before the Lord and focus your mind on Him. Ask Him to speak to you. Let Him know that you are ready to listen to Him, to learn from Him, and to respond to whatever He says to you through His Word.

LISTENING TO GOD

Read and meditate on a passage in the Word of God. (If you do not have a Bible reading plan, you may want to use the 30-day plan suggested on page 8 of this journal.) Ask the Spirit of God to illumine the Scripture to your understanding and apply it to your life. As you read, look for the following:

Observations—*What does this passage say?* Use this space to record observations about your Scripture reading. Summarize or paraphrase the passage. Identify key facts, themes, or characters.

Interpretation—*What does this passage mean?* What does this passage reveal about God and His ways, about man, about Christ, about salvation, about the Christian life, etc.? Are there any promises to claim, commands to obey, examples to follow, or sins to avoid?

ALL QUOTES ARE TAKEN FROM *A PLACE OF QUIET REST* BY NANCY LEIGH DEMOSS.

Application—*What should I do?* In light of what God has revealed, how should you respond? What changes need to be made in your life? How can this passage be practically applied to your life?

(Chapter 9 of *A Place of Quiet Rest*—"Getting the Word into You"—expands on how to look for observations, interpretation, and applications, and includes additional suggestions for how to read and study the Bible.)

RESPONDING TO GOD

You may be familiar with the acrostic *A-C-T-S*. It is a helpful tool for responding to God in praise and prayer.

Adoration—Worship God for Who He is. Focus on various ones of His attributes (holiness, mercy, majesty, omnipotence, etc.) that are revealed in His Word.

Confession—Agree with God about anything He has revealed in your life that is not pleasing to Him. Receive the forgiveness that He has provided through the sacrifice of Christ on the cross.

Thanksgiving—Thank God for what He has done, for His gifts, and for how He has spoken to you through His Word.

Supplication—Bring your requests to Him, both for your own needs and for the needs of others (intercession). Ask Him for grace to obey His Word.

(Chapters 10 and 11 of *A Place of Quiet Rest* have many suggestions on how to respond to God through praise and prayer.)

Remember, this journal is intended to be a tool; don't get hung up on the mechanics. The goal is not to fill in every line in this journal or even to write something in every section. The point is to get into the Word and get the Word into you.

Keep in mind that it is not enough to just read the Bible. The object is that the words that are printed on the page will become indelibly written on your heart, and that you will come to know God intimately and reflect His heart and ways to others.

Suggested Scripture Readings

If you don't already have a Scripture reading plan, here's one you may want to use for the next 30 days. The journey through the Gospel of Mark will give you a fresh glimpse of the Savior and His redemptive life and ministry. Reading three of Paul's epistles will help you understand how to live as a redeemed child of God.

_____ Day 1: Mark 1

_____ Day 2: Mark 2

_____ Day 3: Mark 3

_____ Day 4: Mark 4

_____ Day 5: Mark 5

_____ Day 6: Mark 6

_____ Day 7: Mark 7

_____ Day 8: Mark 8

_____ Day 9: Mark 9

_____ Day 10: Mark 10

_____ Day 11: Mark 11

_____ Day 12: Mark 12

_____ Day 13: Mark 13

_____ Day 14: Mark 14

_____ Day 15: Mark 15

_____ Day 16: Mark 16

_____ Day 17: Ephesians 1

_____ Day 18: Ephesians 2

_____ Day 19: Ephesians 3

_____ Day 20: Ephesians 4

_____ Day 21: Ephesians 5

_____ Day 22: Ephesians 6

_____ Day 23: Philippians 1

_____ Day 24: Philippians 2

_____ Day 25: Philippians 3

_____ Day 26: Philippians 4

_____ Day 27: Colossians 1

_____ Day 28: Colossians 2

_____ Day 29: Colossians 3

_____ Day 30: Colossians 4

Day 1

"I must make a deliberate, daily choice to sit at His feet, to listen to His Word, to receive His love, to let Him change me."

DATE: _____

Preparing My Heart

As you begin, take a moment to quiet your heart before the Lord and focus on Him. Ask Him to speak to you. Let Him know that you are willing to listen and learn from Him through His Word.

Listening to God

SCRIPTURE PASSAGE: _____

Observations: *What does this passage say?* _____

_____

_____

_____

_____

_____

_____

_____

Interpretation: *What does it mean?* _____

_____

_____

_____

_____

_____

_____

_____

_____

Application: *What should I do?* _____

_____

_____

_____

_____

_____

_____

_____

_____

_____

Responding to God

Adoration

_____

_____

_____

_____

_____

_____

_____

Confession

_____

_____

_____

_____

_____

_____

_____

Thanksgiving

_____

_____

_____

_____

_____

_____

_____

Supplication _____

_____

_____

_____

_____

_____

TAKE-AWAY THOUGHT

What key verse or insight will you take with you into your day?

_____

_____

_____

_____

_____

_____

_____

_____

_____

_____

Day 2

"Developing intimacy with the Lord requires a conscious choice. It is a choice to put Him first, above all other responsibilities and tasks."

DATE: _____

PREPARING MY HEART

As you begin, take a moment to quiet your heart before the Lord and focus on Him. Ask Him to speak to you. Let Him know that you are willing to listen and learn from Him through His Word.

LISTENING TO GOD

SCRIPTURE PASSAGE: _____

Observations: *What does this passage say?* _____

_____

_____

_____

_____

_____

_____

_____

Interpretation: *What does it mean?* _____

_____

_____

_____

_____

_____

_____

_____

_____

Application: *What should I do?* _____

_____

_____

_____

_____

_____

_____

_____

_____

Responding to God

Adoration

_____

_____

_____

_____

_____

_____

_____

Confession

_____

_____

_____

_____

_____

_____

_____

Thanksgiving

_____

_____

_____

_____

_____

_____

_____

Supplication _____

_____

_____

_____

_____

_____

_____

TAKE-AWAY THOUGHT

What key verse or insight will you take with you into your day?

_____

_____

_____

_____

_____

_____

_____

_____

_____

_____

Day 3

"In the Scriptures we encounter a God who moves toward us, who seeks to draw us to Himself, and who invites us to know Him in the same way."

DATE: _____

PREPARING MY HEART

As you begin, take a moment to quiet your heart before the Lord and focus on Him. Ask Him to speak to you. Let Him know that you are willing to listen and learn from Him through His Word.

LISTENING TO GOD

SCRIPTURE PASSAGE: _____

Observations: *What does this passage say?* _____

_____

_____

_____

_____

_____

_____

Interpretation: *What does it mean?* _____

_____

_____

_____

_____

_____

_____

_____

Application: *What should I do?* _____

_____

_____

_____

_____

_____

_____

_____

Responding to God

Adoration

_____

_____

_____

_____

_____

_____

_____

Confession

_____

_____

_____

_____

_____

_____

Thanksgiving

_____

_____

_____

_____

_____

_____

Supplication

_____

_____

_____

_____

_____

_____

TAKE-AWAY THOUGHT

What key verse or insight will you take with you into your day?

_____

_____

_____

_____

_____

_____

_____

_____

_____

_____

Day 4

"Spending time with God is more necessary than anything else you or I do on a daily basis, including eating, sleeping, getting dressed, and going to work."

DATE: _____

PREPARING MY HEART

As you begin, take a moment to quiet your heart before the Lord and focus on Him. Ask Him to speak to you. Let Him know that you are willing to listen and learn from Him through His Word.

LISTENING TO GOD

SCRIPTURE PASSAGE: _____

Observations: *What does this passage say?* _____

_____

_____

_____

_____

_____

_____

_____

Interpretation: *What does it mean?* _____

_____

_____

_____

_____

_____

_____

_____

_____

Application: *What should I do?* _____

_____

_____

_____

_____

_____

_____

_____

_____

_____

RESPONDING TO GOD

Adoration

Confession

Thanksgiving

Supplication

Take-Away Thought

What key verse or insight will you take with you into your day?

Day 5

"Are you spiritually dry and thirsty? Begin to praise the Lord and He will fill you with Himself until your thirst is quenched and your cup overflows."

DATE: _____

PREPARING MY HEART

As you begin, take a moment to quiet your heart before the Lord and focus on Him. Ask Him to speak to you. Let Him know that you are willing to listen and learn from Him through His Word.

LISTENING TO GOD

SCRIPTURE PASSAGE: _____

Observations: *What does this passage say?* _____

_____

_____

_____

_____

_____

_____

_____

Interpretation: *What does it mean?* _____

_____

_____

_____

_____

_____

_____

_____

_____

_____

Application: *What should I do?* _____

_____

_____

_____

_____

_____

_____

_____

_____

_____

RESPONDING TO GOD

Adoration _____

_____

_____

_____

_____

_____

_____

Confession _____

_____

_____

_____

_____

_____

_____

Thanksgiving _____

_____

_____

_____

_____

_____

_____

Supplication

_____

_____

_____

_____

_____

_____

TAKE-AWAY THOUGHT

What key verse or insight will you take with you into your day?

_____

_____

_____

_____

_____

_____

_____

_____

_____

_____

Day 6

> *" 'Devotions' is not so much an obligation of the Christian life
> as it is an incredible opportunity to know the God of the universe."*

DATE: _____

Preparing My Heart

As you begin, take a moment to quiet your heart before the Lord and focus on Him. Ask Him to speak to you. Let Him know that you are willing to listen and learn from Him through His Word.

Listening to God

Scripture Passage: _____

Observations: *What does this passage say?* _____

_____

_____

_____

_____

_____

_____

_____

Interpretation: *What does it mean?* _____

_____

_____

_____

_____

_____

_____

_____

_____

Application: *What should I do?* _____

_____

_____

_____

_____

_____

_____

_____

_____

RESPONDING TO GOD

Adoration _____

_____

_____

_____

_____

_____

_____

Confession _____

_____

_____

_____

_____

_____

_____

Thanksgiving _____

_____

_____

_____

_____

_____

_____

Supplication _____

_____

_____

_____

_____

_____

_____

TAKE-AWAY THOUGHT

What key verse or insight will you take with you into your day?

_____

_____

_____

_____

_____

_____

_____

_____

_____

_____

_____

Day 7

"If you are His child, there is within you something that will never be satisfied with anything less than intimate fellowship with your Creator, Redeemer, and heavenly Father."

DATE: _____

PREPARING MY HEART

As you begin, take a moment to quiet your heart before the Lord and focus on Him. Ask Him to speak to you. Let Him know that you are willing to listen and learn from Him through His Word.

LISTENING TO GOD

SCRIPTURE PASSAGE: _____

Observations: *What does this passage say?* _____

_____

_____

_____

_____

_____

_____

_____

Interpretation: *What does it mean?* _____

_____

_____

_____

_____

_____

_____

_____

_____

Application: *What should I do?* _____

_____

_____

_____

_____

_____

_____

_____

_____

RESPONDING TO GOD

Adoration _____

_____

_____

_____

_____

_____

_____

Confession _____

_____

_____

_____

_____

_____

_____

Thanksgiving _____

_____

_____

_____

_____

_____

_____

Supplication

_____

_____

_____

_____

_____

_____

TAKE-AWAY THOUGHT

What key verse or insight will you take with you into your day?

_____

_____

_____

_____

_____

_____

_____

_____

_____

Day 8

*"He has issued to you and me an invitation to
draw near to Him, to walk right into the 'Holy of Holies,'
to enter into an intimate love relationship with Him."*

DATE: _____

PREPARING MY HEART

As you begin, take a moment to quiet your heart before the Lord and focus on Him. Ask Him to speak to you. Let Him know that you are willing to listen and learn from Him through His Word.

LISTENING TO GOD

SCRIPTURE PASSAGE: _____

Observations: *What does this passage say?* _____

_____

_____

_____

_____

_____

_____

_____

Interpretation: *What does it mean?* _____

_____

_____

_____

_____

_____

_____

_____

_____

Application: *What should I do?* _____

_____

_____

_____

_____

_____

_____

_____

_____

_____

RESPONDING TO GOD

Adoration

_____

_____

_____

_____

_____

_____

Confession

_____

_____

_____

_____

_____

_____

Thanksgiving

_____

_____

_____

_____

_____

Supplication _____

_____

_____

_____

_____

_____

_____

TAKE-AWAY THOUGHT

What key verse or insight will you take with you into your day?

_____

_____

_____

_____

_____

_____

_____

_____

_____

_____

Day 9

*"Not until we make pursuing God our highest priority and goal in life
will we begin to fulfill the purpose for which He created us."*

DATE: _____

PREPARING MY HEART

*As you begin, take a moment to quiet your heart before the Lord and focus on Him. Ask Him to
speak to you. Let Him know that you are willing to listen and learn from Him through His Word.*

LISTENING TO GOD

SCRIPTURE PASSAGE: _____

Observations: *What does this passage say?* _____

_____

_____

_____

_____

_____

_____

_____

Interpretation: *What does it mean?* _____

_____

_____

_____

_____

_____

_____

_____

_____

Application: *What should I do?* _____

_____

_____

_____

_____

_____

_____

_____

_____

_____

Responding to God

Adoration

_____

_____

_____

_____

_____

_____

Confession

_____

_____

_____

_____

_____

_____

Thanksgiving

_____

_____

_____

_____

_____

_____

Supplication

_____

TAKE-AWAY THOUGHT

What key verse or insight will you take with you into your day?

Day 10

> *"God never intended that we should merely get into His Word—*
> *His intent is that the Word should get into us."*

DATE: _____

PREPARING MY HEART

As you begin, take a moment to quiet your heart before the Lord and focus on Him. Ask Him to speak to you. Let Him know that you are willing to listen and learn from Him through His Word.

LISTENING TO GOD

SCRIPTURE PASSAGE: _____

Observations: *What does this passage say?* _____

_____

_____

_____

_____

_____

_____

_____

Interpretation: *What does it mean?* _____

_____

_____

_____

_____

_____

_____

_____

_____

Application: *What should I do?* _____

_____

_____

_____

_____

_____

_____

_____

_____

RESPONDING TO GOD

Adoration

_____

_____

_____

_____

_____

_____

_____

Confession

_____

_____

_____

_____

_____

_____

_____

Thanksgiving

_____

_____

_____

_____

_____

_____

_____

Supplication _____

_____

_____

_____

_____

_____

TAKE-AWAY THOUGHT

What key verse or insight will you take with you into your day?

_____

_____

_____

_____

_____

_____

_____

_____

_____

Day 11

*"God's willingness to share the secrets of His heart with His creatures
is just another evidence of His desire to have an intimate relationship with us."*

DATE: _____

PREPARING MY HEART

*As you begin, take a moment to quiet your heart before the Lord and focus on Him. Ask Him to
speak to you. Let Him know that you are willing to listen and learn from Him through His Word.*

LISTENING TO GOD

SCRIPTURE PASSAGE: _____

Observations: *What does this passage say?* _____

_____

_____

_____

_____

_____

_____

_____

Interpretation: *What does it mean?* _____

_____

_____

_____

_____

_____

_____

_____

_____

Application: *What should I do?* _____

_____

_____

_____

_____

_____

_____

_____

_____

RESPONDING TO GOD

Adoration

Confession

Thanksgiving

Supplication

_____

_____

_____

_____

_____

_____

TAKE-AWAY THOUGHT

What key verse or insight will you take with you into your day?

_____

_____

_____

_____

_____

_____

_____

_____

_____

_____

Day 12

"For Jesus, time alone with God was not an option. It was His lifeline to the Father. It was the highest priority of His life."

DATE: _____

PREPARING MY HEART

As you begin, take a moment to quiet your heart before the Lord and focus on Him. Ask Him to speak to you. Let Him know that you are willing to listen and learn from Him through His Word.

LISTENING TO GOD

SCRIPTURE PASSAGE: _____

Observations: *What does this passage say?* _____

_____

_____

_____

_____

_____

_____

_____

Interpretation: *What does it mean?* _____

_____

_____

_____

_____

_____

_____

_____

_____

Application: *What should I do?* _____

_____

_____

_____

_____

_____

_____

_____

_____

_____

RESPONDING TO GOD

Adoration

_____

_____

_____

_____

_____

_____

Confession

_____

_____

_____

_____

_____

_____

Thanksgiving

_____

_____

_____

_____

_____

_____

Supplication

TAKE-AWAY THOUGHT

What key verse or insight will you take with you into your day?

Day 13

"During our quiet time, we enter into His presence and lay our lives before Him. Then with His Word open before us and our hearts lifted up to Him, we listen and seek to discover His heart on the matter."

DATE: _____

PREPARING MY HEART

As you begin, take a moment to quiet your heart before the Lord and focus on Him. Ask Him to speak to you. Let Him know that you are willing to listen and learn from Him through His Word.

LISTENING TO GOD

SCRIPTURE PASSAGE: _____

Observations: *What does this passage say?* _____

_____

_____

_____

_____

_____

_____

_____

Interpretation: *What does it mean?* _____

_____

_____

_____

_____

_____

_____

_____

_____

Application: *What should I do?* _____

_____

_____

_____

_____

_____

_____

_____

_____

RESPONDING TO GOD

Adoration

_____

_____

_____

_____

_____

_____

_____

Confession

_____

_____

_____

_____

_____

_____

_____

Thanksgiving

_____

_____

_____

_____

_____

_____

_____

Supplication _____

_____

_____

_____

_____

_____

TAKE-AWAY THOUGHT

What key verse or insight will you take with you into your day?

_____

_____

_____

_____

_____

_____

_____

_____

_____

_____

Day 14

"As part of a community of faith, we need times to worship, pray, and seek the Lord in the company of God's people. But we must also have times that are set apart to be alone with Him."

DATE: _____

PREPARING MY HEART

As you begin, take a moment to quiet your heart before the Lord and focus on Him. Ask Him to speak to you. Let Him know that you are willing to listen and learn from Him through His Word.

LISTENING TO GOD

SCRIPTURE PASSAGE: _____

Observations: *What does this passage say?* _____

_____

_____

_____

_____

_____

_____

Interpretation: *What does it mean?* _____

_____

_____

_____

_____

_____

_____

_____

_____

_____

Application: *What should I do?* _____

_____

_____

_____

_____

_____

_____

_____

_____

_____

RESPONDING TO GOD

Adoration

_____

_____

_____

_____

_____

_____

Confession

_____

_____

_____

_____

_____

_____

Thanksgiving

_____

_____

_____

_____

_____

_____

Supplication _____

_____

_____

_____

_____

_____

_____

TAKE-AWAY THOUGHT

What key verse or insight will you take with you into your day?

_____

_____

_____

_____

_____

_____

_____

_____

_____

_____

Day 15

"How grateful I am for a merciful, long-suffering heavenly Father who never stops pursuing a love relationship with those who belong to Him."

DATE: _____

PREPARING MY HEART

As you begin, take a moment to quiet your heart before the Lord and focus on Him. Ask Him to speak to you. Let Him know that you are willing to listen and learn from Him through His Word.

LISTENING TO GOD

SCRIPTURE PASSAGE: _____

Observations: *What does this passage say?* _____

_____

_____

_____

_____

_____

_____

_____

Interpretation: *What does it mean?* _____

_____

_____

_____

_____

_____

_____

_____

_____

Application: *What should I do?* _____

_____

_____

_____

_____

_____

_____

_____

_____

_____

RESPONDING TO GOD

Adoration _____

_____

_____

_____

_____

_____

_____

_____

Confession _____

_____

_____

_____

_____

_____

_____

_____

Thanksgiving _____

_____

_____

_____

_____

_____

_____

_____

Supplication _____

_____

_____

_____

_____

_____

TAKE-AWAY THOUGHT

What key verse or insight will you take with you into your day?

_____

_____

_____

_____

_____

_____

_____

_____

_____

Day 16

"The most important purpose of a daily devotional life is not so that we can check another task off our 'to do' list, but rather, that we might experience intimate union and communion with God."

DATE: _____

PREPARING MY HEART

As you begin, take a moment to quiet your heart before the Lord and focus on Him. Ask Him to speak to you. Let Him know that you are willing to listen and learn from Him through His Word.

LISTENING TO GOD

SCRIPTURE PASSAGE: _____

Observations: *What does this passage say?* _____

_____

_____

_____

_____

_____

_____

_____

Interpretation: *What does it mean?*

_____

_____

_____

_____

_____

_____

_____

_____

_____

_____

Application: *What should I do?*

_____

_____

_____

_____

_____

_____

_____

_____

_____

_____

Responding to God

Adoration

_____

_____

_____

_____

_____

_____

Confession

_____

_____

_____

_____

_____

_____

Thanksgiving

_____

_____

_____

_____

_____

_____

Supplication _____

_____

_____

_____

_____

_____

TAKE-AWAY THOUGHT

What key verse or insight will you take with you into your day?

_____

_____

_____

_____

_____

_____

_____

_____

_____

Day 17

*"I have come to believe that it is absolutely impossible for me to cultivate
an intimate relationship with God, or to become the woman He wants me to be,
apart from spending daily time alone with Him."*

DATE: _____

PREPARING MY HEART

*As you begin, take a moment to quiet your heart before the Lord and focus on Him. Ask Him to
speak to you. Let Him know that you are willing to listen and learn from Him through His Word.*

LISTENING TO GOD

SCRIPTURE PASSAGE: _____

Observations: *What does this passage say?* _____

_____

_____

_____

_____

_____

_____

_____

Interpretation: *What does it mean?*

Application: *What should I do?*

RESPONDING TO GOD

Adoration

_____

_____

_____

_____

_____

_____

Confession

_____

_____

_____

_____

_____

_____

Thanksgiving

_____

_____

_____

_____

_____

_____

Supplication _____

_____

_____

_____

_____

_____

TAKE-AWAY THOUGHT

What key verse or insight will you take with you into your day?

_____

_____

_____

_____

_____

_____

_____

_____

_____

_____

Day 18

"There is no substitute for spending consistent, quality time alone in His presence. The cost is great. But the rewards are even greater."

DATE: _____

PREPARING MY HEART

As you begin, take a moment to quiet your heart before the Lord and focus on Him. Ask Him to speak to you. Let Him know that you are willing to listen and learn from Him through His Word.

LISTENING TO GOD

SCRIPTURE PASSAGE: _____

Observations: *What does this passage say?* _____

_____

_____

_____

_____

_____

_____

_____

Interpretation: *What does it mean?*

Application: *What should I do?*

RESPONDING TO GOD

Adoration

_____

_____

_____

_____

_____

_____

_____

Confession

_____

_____

_____

_____

_____

_____

_____

Thanksgiving

_____

_____

_____

_____

_____

_____

Supplication _____

_____

_____

_____

_____

_____

_____

TAKE-AWAY THOUGHT

What key verse or insight will you take with you into your day?

_____

_____

_____

_____

_____

_____

_____

_____

_____

_____

Day 19

"If you have walked with God for any length of time, you know what it is to have a breach in the relationship. The purpose of a daily devotional time is to get back into His presence, to find out what has caused the breach, and to reestablish fellowship."

DATE: _____

PREPARING MY HEART

As you begin, take a moment to quiet your heart before the Lord and focus on Him. Ask Him to speak to you. Let Him know that you are willing to listen and learn from Him through His Word.

LISTENING TO GOD

SCRIPTURE PASSAGE: _____

Observations: *What does this passage say?* _____

_____

_____

_____

_____

_____

_____

_____

Interpretation: *What does it mean?* _____

_____

_____

_____

_____

_____

_____

_____

_____

_____

Application: *What should I do?* _____

_____

_____

_____

_____

_____

_____

_____

_____

_____

RESPONDING TO GOD

Adoration

_____

_____

_____

_____

_____

_____

_____

Confession

_____

_____

_____

_____

_____

_____

_____

Thanksgiving

_____

_____

_____

_____

_____

_____

Supplication

What key verse or insight will you take with you into your day?

Day 20

"Nothing can compare to the joy and privilege of sitting and learning at the feet of our heavenly Master."

DATE: _____

PREPARING MY HEART

As you begin, take a moment to quiet your heart before the Lord and focus on Him. Ask Him to speak to you. Let Him know that you are willing to listen and learn from Him through His Word.

LISTENING TO GOD

SCRIPTURE PASSAGE: _____

Observations: *What does this passage say?* _____

_____

_____

_____

_____

_____

_____

_____

Interpretation: *What does it mean?*

Application: *What should I do?*

RESPONDING TO GOD

Adoration

Confession

Thanksgiving

Supplication

_____

_____

_____

_____

_____

_____

TAKE-AWAY THOUGHT

What key verse or insight will you take with you into your day?

_____

_____

_____

_____

_____

_____

_____

_____

_____

Day 21

"As we spend time alone with God, our lives are brought into submission to God and His will."

DATE: _____

PREPARING MY HEART

As you begin, take a moment to quiet your heart before the Lord and focus on Him. Ask Him to speak to you. Let Him know that you are willing to listen and learn from Him through His Word.

LISTENING TO GOD

SCRIPTURE PASSAGE: _____

Observations: *What does this passage say?* _____

_____

_____

_____

_____

_____

_____

_____

Interpretation: *What does it mean?* _____

_____

_____

_____

_____

_____

_____

_____

_____

Application: *What should I do?* _____

_____

_____

_____

_____

_____

_____

_____

_____

RESPONDING TO GOD

Adoration _____

_____

_____

_____

_____

_____

Confession _____

_____

_____

_____

_____

_____

Thanksgiving _____

_____

_____

_____

_____

_____

Supplication _____

_____

_____

_____

_____

_____

TAKE-AWAY THOUGHT

What key verse or insight will you take with you into your day?

_____

_____

_____

_____

_____

_____

_____

_____

_____

Day 22

> *"God desires to have the kind of relationship with us where we are quick to seek His counsel and direction in relation to the matters that concern us."*

DATE: _____

Preparing My Heart

As you begin, take a moment to quiet your heart before the Lord and focus on Him. Ask Him to speak to you. Let Him know that you are willing to listen and learn from Him through His Word.

Listening to God

SCRIPTURE PASSAGE: _____

Observations: *What does this passage say?* _____

_____

_____

_____

_____

_____

_____

_____

Interpretation: *What does it mean?* _____

_____

_____

_____

_____

_____

_____

_____

_____

Application: *What should I do?* _____

_____

_____

_____

_____

_____

_____

_____

_____

RESPONDING TO GOD

Adoration _____

_____

_____

_____

_____

_____

_____

Confession _____

_____

_____

_____

_____

_____

_____

Thanksgiving _____

_____

_____

_____

_____

_____

_____

Supplication

_____

_____

_____

_____

_____

_____

TAKE-AWAY THOUGHT

What key verse or insight will you take with you into your day?

_____

_____

_____

_____

_____

_____

_____

_____

_____

Day 23

*"You may be a seasoned student of the Word. You may even be a Bible study leader. But if your study of the Word does not lead you to **know** God, you have missed the whole purpose."*

DATE: _____

PREPARING MY HEART

As you begin, take a moment to quiet your heart before the Lord and focus on Him. Ask Him to speak to you. Let Him know that you are willing to listen and learn from Him through His Word.

LISTENING TO GOD

SCRIPTURE PASSAGE: _____

Observations: *What does this passage say?* _____

_____

_____

_____

_____

_____

_____

_____

Interpretation: *What does it mean?* _____

_____

_____

_____

_____

_____

_____

_____

_____

_____

Application: *What should I do?* _____

_____

_____

_____

_____

_____

_____

_____

_____

_____

_____

RESPONDING TO GOD

Adoration

Confession

Thanksgiving

Supplication

_____

_____

_____

_____

_____

_____

TAKE-AWAY THOUGHT

What key verse or insight will you take with you into your day?

_____

_____

_____

_____

_____

_____

_____

_____

_____

_____

Day 24

"Day after day, as I open my heart to His light, He is faithful to bring to my attention that which has grieved Him."

DATE: _____

Preparing My Heart

As you begin, take a moment to quiet your heart before the Lord and focus on Him. Ask Him to speak to you. Let Him know that you are willing to listen and learn from Him through His Word.

Listening to God

SCRIPTURE PASSAGE: _____

Observations: *What does this passage say?* _____

_____

_____

_____

_____

_____

_____

_____

Interpretation: *What does it mean?* _____

_____

_____

_____

_____

_____

_____

_____

_____

_____

Application: *What should I do?* _____

_____

_____

_____

_____

_____

_____

_____

_____

_____

RESPONDING TO GOD

Adoration

_____

_____

_____

_____

_____

_____

_____

Confession

_____

_____

_____

_____

_____

_____

_____

Thanksgiving

_____

_____

_____

_____

_____

_____

_____

Supplication

_____

_____

_____

_____

_____

_____

_____

TAKE-AWAY THOUGHT

What key verse or insight will you take with you into your day?

_____

_____

_____

_____

_____

_____

_____

_____

_____

_____

Day 25

"As you begin spending time each day looking into the face of Jesus, beholding Him, and listening to His voice, you will find that your life will be transfigured from the inside out."

DATE: _____

PREPARING MY HEART

As you begin, take a moment to quiet your heart before the Lord and focus on Him. Ask Him to speak to you. Let Him know that you are willing to listen and learn from Him through His Word.

LISTENING TO GOD

SCRIPTURE PASSAGE: _____

Observations: *What does this passage say?* _____

_____

_____

_____

_____

_____

_____

_____

Interpretation: *What does it mean?* _____

_____

_____

_____

_____

_____

_____

_____

_____

Application: *What should I do?* _____

_____

_____

_____

_____

_____

_____

_____

_____

_____

RESPONDING TO GOD

Adoration

Confession

Thanksgiving

Supplication _____

_____

_____

_____

_____

_____

TAKE-AWAY THOUGHT

What key verse or insight will you take with you into your day?

_____

_____

_____

_____

_____

_____

_____

_____

Day 26

> *"If we fail to stop and draw from His fresh, infinite supply of
> mercy and grace, we will find ourselves having to operate out of our
> own depleted, meager resources."*

DATE: _____

PREPARING MY HEART

As you begin, take a moment to quiet your heart before the Lord and focus on Him. Ask Him to
speak to you. Let Him know that you are willing to listen and learn from Him through His Word.

LISTENING TO GOD

SCRIPTURE PASSAGE: _____

Observations: *What does this passage say?* _____

_____

_____

_____

_____

_____

_____

Interpretation: *What does it mean?* _____

_____

_____

_____

_____

_____

_____

_____

Application: *What should I do?* _____

_____

_____

_____

_____

_____

_____

_____

_____

Responding to God

Adoration

_____

_____

_____

_____

_____

_____

Confession

_____

_____

_____

_____

_____

_____

Thanksgiving

_____

_____

_____

_____

_____

Supplication _____

_____

_____

_____

_____

_____

TAKE-AWAY THOUGHT

What key verse or insight will you take with you into your day?

_____

_____

_____

_____

_____

_____

_____

_____

_____

_____

_____

Day 27

"It is in those daily devotional times alone with Him that He calms my spirit, slows down my racing pulse, and gives me perspective and renewed desire and strength to serve Him another day."

DATE: _____

PREPARING MY HEART

As you begin, take a moment to quiet your heart before the Lord and focus on Him. Ask Him to speak to you. Let Him know that you are willing to listen and learn from Him through His Word.

LISTENING TO GOD

SCRIPTURE PASSAGE: _____

Observations: *What does this passage say?* _____

_____

_____

_____

_____

_____

_____

_____

Interpretation: *What does it mean?*

Application: *What should I do?*

Responding to God

Adoration

Confession

Thanksgiving

Supplication

Take-Away Thought

What key verse or insight will you take with you into your day?

Day 28

"Knowing the tendency of my heart to want its own will, I make it a practice to kneel before the Lord at least once each day. In doing so, I acknowledge that He is my Lord and I am His servant."

DATE: _____

PREPARING MY HEART

As you begin, take a moment to quiet your heart before the Lord and focus on Him. Ask Him to speak to you. Let Him know that you are willing to listen and learn from Him through His Word.

LISTENING TO GOD

SCRIPTURE PASSAGE: _____

Observations: *What does this passage say?* _____

_____

_____

_____

_____

_____

_____

_____

Interpretation: *What does it mean?* _____

_____

_____

_____

_____

_____

_____

_____

_____

_____

Application: *What should I do?* _____

_____

_____

_____

_____

_____

_____

_____

_____

_____

RESPONDING TO GOD

Adoration

_____

_____

_____

_____

_____

_____

Confession

_____

_____

_____

_____

_____

_____

_____

Thanksgiving

_____

_____

_____

_____

_____

_____

Supplication

_____

_____

_____

_____

_____

_____

TAKE-AWAY THOUGHT

What key verse or insight will you take with you into your day?

_____

_____

_____

_____

_____

_____

_____

_____

_____

Day 29

"Time spent alone with Jesus each day will order our hearts and grant a sense of direction."

DATE: _____

PREPARING MY HEART

As you begin, take a moment to quiet your heart before the Lord and focus on Him. Ask Him to speak to you. Let Him know that you are willing to listen and learn from Him through His Word.

LISTENING TO GOD

SCRIPTURE PASSAGE: _____

Observations: *What does this passage say?* _____

_____

_____

_____

_____

_____

_____

_____

Interpretation: *What does it mean?* _____

_____

_____

_____

_____

_____

_____

_____

_____

Application: *What should I do?* _____

_____

_____

_____

_____

_____

_____

_____

_____

_____

RESPONDING TO GOD

Adoration _____

_____

_____

_____

_____

_____

_____

Confession _____

_____

_____

_____

_____

_____

_____

Thanksgiving _____

_____

_____

_____

_____

_____

Supplication

_____

_____

_____

_____

_____

_____

TAKE-AWAY THOUGHT

What key verse or insight will you take with you into your day?

_____

_____

_____

_____

_____

_____

_____

_____

_____

_____

Day 30

"As you walk in union and communion with Him, a sweet fragrance will be released and luscious fruit will be born —the fragrance and the fruit of His Spirit."

DATE: _____

Preparing My Heart

As you begin, take a moment to quiet your heart before the Lord and focus on Him. Ask Him to speak to you. Let Him know that you are willing to listen and learn from Him through His Word.

Listening to God

SCRIPTURE PASSAGE: _____

Observations: *What does this passage say?* _____

_____

_____

_____

_____

_____

_____

_____

Interpretation: *What does it mean?* _____

_____

_____

_____

_____

_____

_____

_____

_____

_____

Application: *What should I do?* _____

_____

_____

_____

_____

_____

_____

_____

_____

_____

_____